Green Iguanas

BY ELIZABETH RAUM

amicus
high interest

Amicus High Interest is an imprint of Amicus
P.O. Box 1329, Mankato, MN 56002
www.amicuspublishing.us

Library of Congress Cataloging-in-Publication Data
Raum, Elizabeth, author.
 Green iguanas / by Elizabeth Raum.
    pages cm. — (Lizards)
 Audience: Grades K to grade 3.
 Summary: "Describes green iguanas, including what they
look like, where they live, some of their behaviors, how they
reproduce, and how they fit in the world"— Provided by
publisher.
 Includes bibliographical references and index.
 ISBN 978-1-60753-487-7 (library binding) —
 ISBN 978-1-60753-700-7 (ebook)
 1. Green iguana—Juvenile literature. I. Title.
 QL666.L25R38 2015
 597.95'42—dc23
                                          2013028240

Editor: Wendy Dieker
Series Designer: Kathleen Petelinsek
Book Designer: Heather Dreisbach
Photo Researcher: Kurtis Kinneman

Photo Credits: Superstock, cover; Dave and Sigrun Tollerton/
Alamy 5; WaterFrame/Alamy 6; FLPA/SuperStock 8–9;
Minden Pictures/SuperStock 11; NHPA/SuperStock 12;
Ernie Janes/Alamy 15; Minden Pictures/SuperStock 16;
Duardo Grund/age fotostock/SuperStock 18–19; Ivan
Kuzmin/imagebrok/imagebroker.net 21; Minden Pictures/
SuperStock 22; age fotostock/SuperStock 25; Minden
Pictures/SuperStock 26; Minden Pictures/SuperStock 29

Printed in the United States of America at Corporate Graphics
in North Mankato, Minnesota.

10 9 8 7 6 5 4 3 2 1

Table of Contents

Dive to Safety

This green iguana spends his time in tree branches high above the river. It munches on leaves. It **basks** in the sunshine. Suddenly, a shadow passes above. It's a hawk! The hawk is ready to attack. The iguana must act quickly! It doesn't want to become the hawk's next meal. Splash! The iguana drops 40 feet (12 m) into the river below.

Green iguanas are not always green. They can change color.

**These big lizards are
good swimmers.**

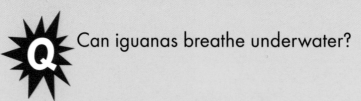 Can iguanas breathe underwater?

The hawk dives toward the water. The iguana ducks below the surface. That's where it stays until the danger has passed. Then the iguana swims to shore. Its long tail swishes back and forth as it speeds toward land. Then it climbs back into the tree. Safe at last!

 No. But they can hold their breath for up to 45 minutes.

A Look at Iguanas

Green iguanas live in rain forests. They live near rivers, lakes, and swamps. The oldest lizards live in high tree branches. Younger ones live in lower branches. Sometimes, they live on the ground. But they still stay by water. You will find green iguanas in Central and South America. They also live on Caribbean islands.

Iguanas live in warm rain forests.

Adult iguanas are 5 to 7 feet (1.5 to 2.1 m) long. They weigh up to 18 pounds (8.2 kg). Soft, leathery scales cover the lizard's body. A flap of skin hangs under their chin. It is called a **dewlap**. A crest begins at the back of its head. Spines run from the crest to the tail.

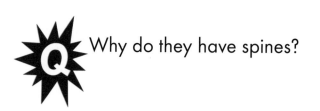
Q Why do they have spines?

Sharp spines form a single line down an iguana's back.

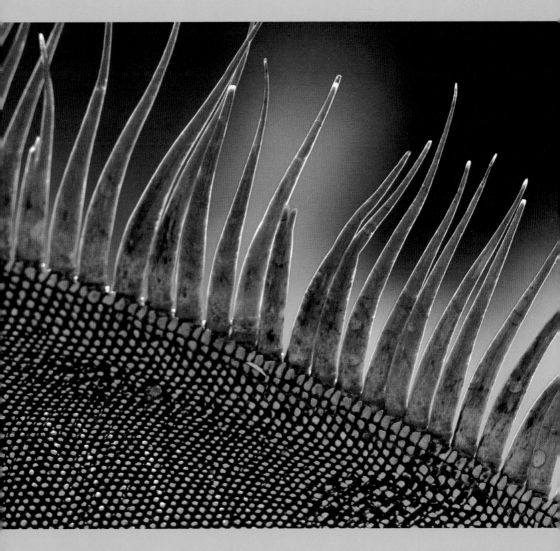

 The spines are sharp. They help fight off **predators**.

Not all green iguanas are green. Older males can be brownish-green. Some even look blue. Green iguanas may change color during the day. When it's cold outside, their skin may look darker. Darker colors take in heat from the sun. The iguanas become lighter when the sun is bright and warm.

Iguanas will change colors as they age. They also change color to warm up or cool down.

Life in the Trees

Most lizards are meat-eaters. Not green iguanas. They are **herbivores**. They eat only plants. They eat leaves and flowers. They also like fruit. Some even eat **algae**. They rarely move, so they need less energy than most lizards. Green iguanas spend their days resting on branches and eating leaves. They get water from the food they eat.

Big green leaves make
a good meal. Yum!

Sharp claws help an iguana climb trees.

Q What happens if an iguana loses its tail?

Green iguanas have five very long toes. Each toe has a sharp claw. They use their toes to climb trees. Their long tails help them balance. The tail also helps them fight enemies. Frightened iguanas usually freeze in place or hide. But if they are attacked, they whip their tails. Enemies grab it, but then the tail falls off. The iguana speeds away.

The tail regrows.

Green iguanas have good eyesight. This helps them see predators. They also have a third eye on the top of their heads. This eye is not an eye that sees well. It only sees shadows. Scientists think it takes in the sun's energy. It may help iguanas know when to bask or mate.

The iguana's keen eyes help them spot danger.

Eggs and Babies

In the spring, males try to attract females. Many become orange. Some bob their heads up and down. They wave their dewlap. Females may bob their heads back to show interest. Males may mate with several females. Females may mate with more than one male. About 65 days later, the female lays eggs.

This male is showing off his colors. He hopes to find a mate.

Iguanas lay their eggs in a hole.

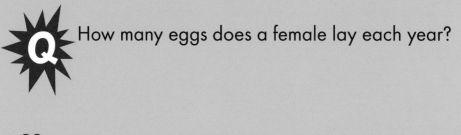

Q How many eggs does a female lay each year?

22

Females travel up to 2 miles (3.2 km) to find a good place to make a nest. They dig a deep hole. They lay the eggs at the bottom. Then they cover them up. Some females guard the nest for several days. But then they leave the nest. They never meet their babies.

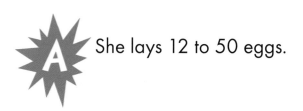

She lays 12 to 50 eggs.

Baby iguanas hatch in 10 to 14 weeks. They are 7 to 10 inches (17.8 to 25.4 cm) long. Their scales are bright green. Newborn iguanas stay together. The group of babies leaves the nest. They climb into the trees. Baby iguanas eat bugs. They also eat the droppings of adult iguanas. Gross!

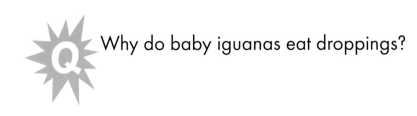 Why do baby iguanas eat droppings?

**Babies are bright green
when they hatch.**

 The droppings have partly **digested** plants.
It might help them get used to eating plants
as they grow.

Watch out, baby! This bird will eat lizards for lunch.

 What does iguana meat taste like?

Staying Alive

Many baby iguanas die. They have many predators. Large birds and crocodiles will eat them. Adult iguanas can get away from other animals. But they can't always get away from people. Pet dealers capture green iguanas to sell as pets. Hunters sell iguana skin for boots, belts, and purses. People eat their meat and eggs, too.

Some say it tastes like chicken. In Spanish, iguanas are called "chicken of the trees."

Loss of their **habitat**, or home, is the biggest problem facing iguanas. People are clearing rain forests. They want to build farms, roads, and towns. Green iguanas need trees to survive. Many **environmental groups** are taking steps to protect the rain forest. They want to protect the animals that live there. That's good news for green iguanas.

Farmers clear trees in the rain forest. This means iguanas may lose their homes.

Glossary

algae Small plants with no roots that grow in water or damp places.

bask To lie in the sun to warm up.

dewlap A flap of skin beneath the chin.

digest To change food into energy.

environmental group An organization that works to protect nature.

habitat The place and natural conditions where an animal lives.

herbivore An animal that eats only plants.

predator An animal that hunts another for food.

Read More

Landau, Elaine. *Your Pet Iguana.* New York: Children's Press, 2007.

Lunis, Natalie. *Green Iguanas.* New York: Bearport Pub., 2010.

Rabe, Tish. *Miles and Miles of Reptiles.* New York: Random House, 2009.

Websites

Green Iguana: Connecticut's Beardsley Zoo
http://www.beardsleyzoo.org/greeniguana-fk1

Green Iguana: National Geographic
http://animals.nationalgeographic.com/animals/reptiles/green-iguana/

Green Iguana Fact Sheet: National Zoo
http://nationalzoo.si.edu/Animals/ReptilesAmphibians/Facts/FactSheets/Greeniguana.cfm

Every effort has been made to ensure that these websites are appropriate for children. However, because of the nature of the Internet, it is impossible to guarantee that these sites will remain active indefinitely or that their contents will not be altered.

Index

About the Author

Elizabeth Raum has worked as a teacher, librarian, and writer. She has written dozens of books for young readers. Elizabeth likes doing research and learning about new topics. She enjoyed learning about lizards. Even so, she doesn't want one for a pet! Dogs and cats are cuddlier. Visit her website at www.elizabethraum.net.